**Yo Adrian!**
There's no stopping NFL running back **Adrian Peterson** when he bursts through the line. Peterson had a monstrous rookie year, rushing for 1,341 yards. In just his eighth game as a pro, he broke the NFL single-game rushing record (296 yards).

# IN YOUR FACE 3-D
## The BEST 3-D BOOK Ever!

| | |
|---|---|
| Stereographer | **David E. Klutho** |
| Designer | **Beth Bugler** |
| 3-D Graphics Designer | **ron labbe, studio 3D** |
| Editor | **Andrea Woo** |
| Photo Editors | **Marguerite Schropp Lucarelli** |
| | **Gina Houseman** |
| Writers | **Jason Plautz** |
| | **Delena Turman** |

## TIME INC. HOME ENTERTAINMENT

Publisher **Richard Fraiman**

General Manager **Steven Sandonato**

Executive Director, Marketing Services **Carol Pittard**

Director, Retail & Special Sales **Tom Mifsud**

Director, New Product Development **Peter Harper**

Assistant Director, Brand Marketing **Laura Adam**

Associate Counsel **Helen Wan**

Senior Brand Manager, TWRS/M **Holly Oakes**

Design & Prepress Manager **Anne-Michelle Gallero**

Book Production Manager **Susan Chodakiewicz**

Brand & Licensing Manager **Alexandra Bliss**

**Special thanks:** Glenn Buonocore, Margaret Hess, Suzanne Janso, Dennis Marcel, Robert Marasco, Brooke Reger, Mary Sarro-Waite, Ilene Schreider, Adriana Tierno, Alex Voznesenskiy,

Copyright 2008 Time Inc. Home Entertainment

Published by SIK Books

Time Inc.
1271 Avenue of the Americas
New York, New York 10020

ISBN 10: 1-60320-027-4
ISBN 13: 978-1-60320-027-1
Library of Congress Control Number: 2008903291

PRINTED IN CHINA

SIK Books is a trademark of Time Inc.

We welcome your comments and suggestions about SIK Books. Please write to us at:

SIK Books
Attention: Book Editors
PO Box 11016
Des Moines, IA 50336-1016

If you would like to order any of our hardcover Collector's Edition books, please call us at 1-800-327-6388. (Monday through Friday, 7:00 a.m.– 8:00 p.m. or Saturday, 7:00 a.m.– 6:00 p.m. Central Time).

**To order replacement 3-D glasses free of charge, please call 1-800-327-6388.**

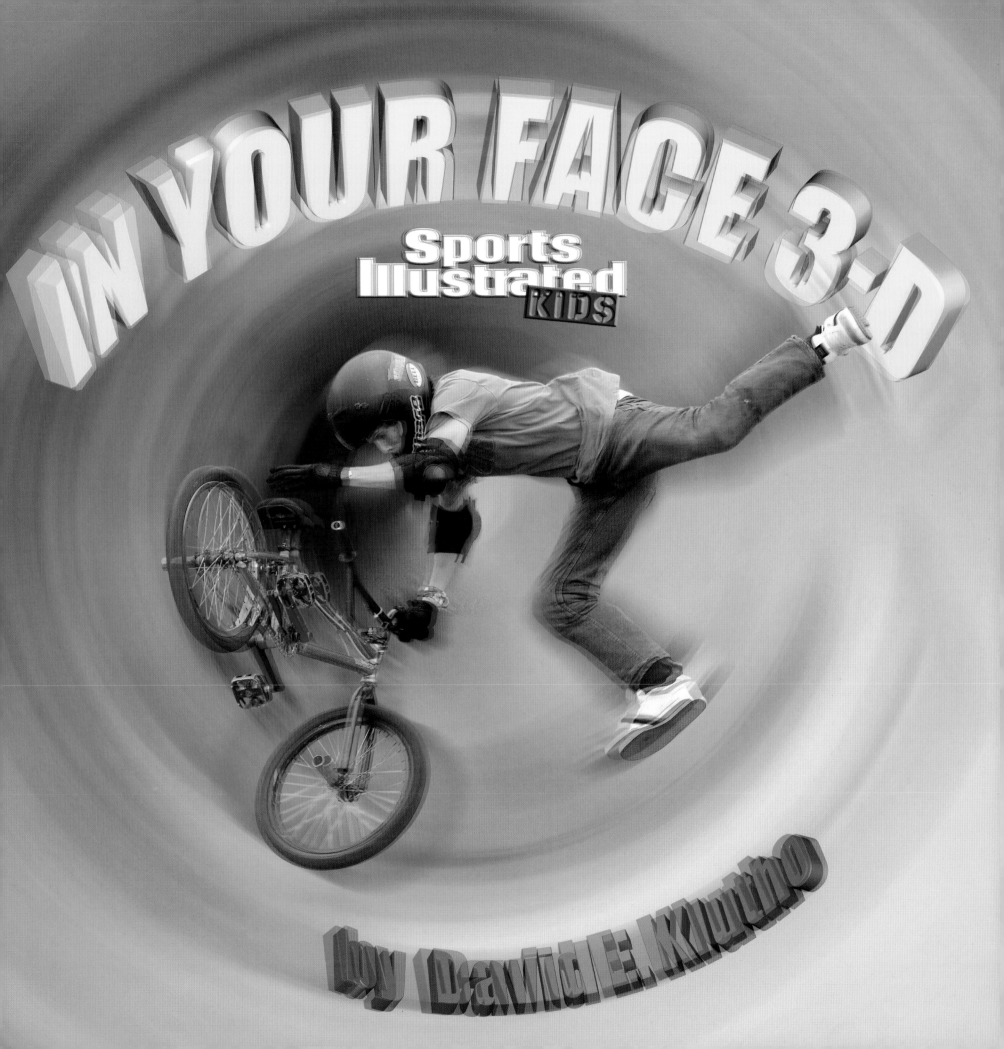

# Welcome . . .

to the amazing world of three-dimensional (3-D) sports photography. This one-of-a-kind project was years in the making. More than 28 different 3-D camera setups were used in creating these unique sports images that have incredible realism and depth. This book is dedicated to the people who believed in and supported my photography from the beginning (when I was in the eighth grade).

**Great thanks to Victor and Joan Klutho, Tony and Marianne Pauly, and John A. Kilo.**

I would like to thank ron labbe of studio 3D for his contributions to this book. Without studio 3D's help, this project would have been impossible. Finally, much of my inspiration for this 3-D creation was gained through my membership in the National Stereoscopic Association (NSA), The New York Stereoscopic Society, and the International Stereoscopic Union (ISU). Thanks to the many members whose friendship and association have given even greater dimension to this book. Put on your 3-D glasses and enjoy!

**David E. Klutho**

# FAST FORWARD

## So, what is this 3D stuff?

Let me ask you this: How many cameras do you have in your head right now? The answer is two! Yes, your eyes are like cameras, and having two means that your brain gets two slightly different pictures of our three-dimensional world. How different? Hold your finger between your eyes and this page, and then close one eye at a time. Does your finger seem to jump back and forth? If you leave your finger there and continue reading, you should notice that your finger becomes doubled. (If you focus on your finger instead, then the book page becomes doubled!)

This difference between what each eye sees is called "parallax." Notice that the pictures in this book are also doubled. When you put on the 3-D glasses, the red lens hides one image, and the blue lens hides the other. Each eye ends up seeing a slightly different picture, just like in real life! This system is called "anaglyph" and it creates the 3-D effect. (You can see more of these anaglyph images online at sikids.com/3d) You need two cameras to take a 3-D picture (or one camera with two lenses). Sports Illustrated photographer David E. Klutho probably has more

3-D camera setups than anyone in the world. Most of his setups are specially built and some are one of a kind. There aren't a lot of 3-D cams out there, and the equipment needed to capture the high-speed action of sports is even more specialized. Few people know the secrets of stereo photography like David does.

3-D pictures have actually been around for a long time. They are still usually shot with film, because digital cameras are not quite ready for 3-D. In fact, the first 3-D pictures were taken prior to the invention of film, in the 1850s, before the Civil War! Back then, pictures were made on metal plates and subjects had to hold very still.

We've come a long way since then. People can now be photographed running, jumping, and even slam dunking. The book in your hands is proof. It represents the state of the art in 3-D publishing, featuring the best 3-D sports pictures — ever!

**ron labbe**
**studio 3D**

## Rock and Roll

**David Chancellor** of So iLL Climbing Holds scales huge rocks without any ropes. Bouldering is extremely dangerous. Luckily for Chancellor, he can practice in the safety of his garage *(below)*.

## △ Practice Makes Perfect

**Danica Patrick** started racing go-karts when she was nine years old. By age 16, she had moved to England to pursue a career in racing. Three years after being named IndyCar Rookie of Year in 2005, Patrick made history, becoming the first female driver to win a race in IndyCar history.

## ◁ Quick Check-Up

Members of **Jimmie Johnson**'s crew make adjustments to his car during practice. Drivers use the practice sessions before a race to dial in their car.

**"I figure practice puts your brains in your muscles."**

— Sam Snead, golfer

**Get Ready. Get Set. Go!**
Triathletes jump into the water for the first leg of a triathlon. A triathlon consists of swimming, biking, and running. USA Triathlon has more than 100,000 members and athletes from the ages of seven to 87 have competed in them.

## Golden Touch

The Notre Dame football team's iconic helmets never lack luster. That's because student managers spray them before each game with paint that contains actual gold dust. The Irish's helmets are a tribute to the famous Golden Dome on campus.

TEAM

WORK

△ **Rush Job**

A crew of six can be over the wall during a pit stop in the Indy Racing League. The mechanics work together to change tires and re-fuel so that the driver can get back to the race as quickly as possible. A typical stop lasts only about 10 seconds!

◁ **Pile Driver**

It took a total team effort from the goal-line defense to prevent this Tennessee touchdown.

**“Michael, if you can’t pass, you can’t play.”**

Coach Dean Smith to Michael Jordan during his freshman year at North Carolina

### Two to Tango

In ice dancing, couples must always be in sync with each other and the music. Artistry and technique are emphasized in the sport, which made its Olympic debut in 1976.

It takes two . . . .

# . . . or 11

**Block Party**
Notre Dame players attempt to block a field goal against one of their fiercest rivals, Michigan. The two powerhouses square off regularly at the beginning of each college football season. The heated rivalry dates back to 1877.

**Up For Grabs**
Players from Southern Illinois and Drake battle for a rebound. One of the greatest rebounders in basketball history, Bill Russell, understood the significance of team. "We never had a person we called a role player," Russell said. "We had people that played on our team and every one of them was important to us."

△ **A Little Help From Friends**
Even a great player has to hand it
off to a teammate sometimes.
New England Patriots quarterback
**Tom Brady** and his team won three
Super Bowls in four seasons.

◁ **Group Mentality**
In cross-country competitions,
teammates often stay in a pack,
which helps keep them motivated
during the long-distance race.

**Goal Oriented**
You can't accuse Team Canada of not knowing how to work together. The Canadians have dominated international hockey in recent years, winning the 2003, '04, and '07 world championship, the 2002 Olympic gold medal, and the 2004 World Cup of Hockey.

**❝The nice thing about teamwork is that you always have others on your side.❞**

— Margaret Carty

## We Got Your Back

The Green Bay Packers take care of business on the field. But they wouldn't be able to do it without the help of the G-Force – the nickname for their die-hard fans. About 73,000 supporters bring energy and life to every game at historic Lambeau Field.

## Splish Splash

It's a wet and wild time for freestyle kayakers. They perform tricks in the waves, including rolls, flips, grinds, and jumps. Sometimes they even find themselves underwater.

# Watch Out!

## ◁ Hang on Tight

If you think doing tricks on a skateboard is tough, imagine what it'd be like if that skateboard were 200 pounds. That's the weight of a motocross bike. Even with all that heavy lifting, motocross riders still perform dangerous stunts and flips in the air.

**Get Inline**
**Demetrius Watson** grinds on a pole, one of the many daredevil tricks in aggressive inline skating. Skaters also do flips, spins, grabs, and slides.

# what we skate on: pipes, rails, steps, benches, curbs . . .

## Wear Your Helmet
Mountain biking is a rough sport. Riders have to navigate rocky terrain, not to mention trees, branches, and streams. The bumpy rides were introduced to the Olympics in 1996.

## Hold that Pose

Photographers have to get up close to the action to capture the best shots. Stereographer David E. Klutho has to avoid everything thing from flying hockey pucks to soaring BMX bikes. Klutho has taken thousands of sports photos, including all the ones in this book.

> **Some people might consider it the Secret Service of bull riding. It's our job to take a hit, if we have to, to keep the bull rider safe.**
>
> — Allan Dessel, Rodeo Clown

### Clowning Around

It's not all funny business for rodeo clowns, who have to distract bulls after riders have been thrown off. While trying to avoid the bull, they are also expected to entertain the crowd.

**Let's Rumble**

Wrestling dates back thousands of years, when it was one of the most popular sports in ancient Greece. Today, the sport has many styles — such as sumo, collegiate, and Greco-Roman.

**Digital Anaglyphic Vertically Inclined Display**

TOOLS OF THE TRADE

**"As a kid, I might have been psycho, I guess, but I used to throw golf balls in the trees and try and somehow make par from them. I thought that was fun."** — Tiger Woods

**My Board Rocks!**
**Nate Holland,** a three-time X Games gold medalist in snowboard cross, shows off his board. Snowboard cross is a crazy fast-paced event in which boarders simultaneously race down a course, oftentimes bumping into each other.

**Alex Delvecchio**
Center
Detroit Red Wings
1951–1974

**Bobby Clarke**
Center
Philadelphia Flyers
1969–1984

**Bobby Hull**
Left Wing
Chicago Blackhawks
1957–1972

**Wayne Gretzky**
Center
Los Angeles Kings
1988–1996

**Sidney Crosby**
Center
Pittsburgh Penguins
2005–present

# Learning Curves

Check out the blades on NHL players' sticks over the years. Bobby Hull's curve was the most extreme when he played for the Chicago Blackhawks. Hull's stick was known to have a banana blade, named for its resemblance to the fruit. Slap shots coming off those curved blades would dip and bend unpredictably and officials feared for the safety of the goalie and fans. The league first instituted rules on stick curves in 1967. Today, a measuring device is used to ensure that the curve is no more than three-quarters of an inch.

**The Crosby Show**
Penguins center **Sidney Crosby** knows how to wield a stick. He is the youngest player to reach 200 career points in NHL history.

MAX. LENGTH OF PLAYER BLADE 12 1/2" (31.75cm)

MAX. WIDTH OF GOAL PADS 11" (27.94cm)
(FOR QUICK REFERENCE ONLY)

MAX. LENGTH OF GOAL BLOCKER 15" (38.10cm)

MAX. LENGTH OF GOAL CATCHER CUFF 8" (20.32cm) AND
MAX. WIDTH OF GOAL BLOCKER 8" (20.32cm)

MAX. LENGTH OF GOAL BLADE 15 1/2" (39.37cm)

MAX. WIDTH, BOTTOM OF HEEL TO TOP OF HEEL (GOAL STICK) 4 1/2" (11.43cm)

MAX. CURVE OF PLAYER BLADE 3/4" (1.91cm)

MIN. WIDTH OF GOAL CATCH GLOVE CUFF 4" (10.16cm)

MAX. WIDTH OF GOAL BLADE / MAX. WIDTH OF GOAL PADDLE 3 1/2" (8.89cm)

MAX. WIDTH OF PLAYER BLADE 3" (7.62cm)

MIN. WIDTH OF PLAYER BLADE 2" (5.08cm)

*Gretzky*

Ne

**Making a Racket**
Most professional tennis players, like **Agnes Szavay** of Hungary, don't play with the same rackets that are sold to the public. The pros heavily customize theirs to add mass and swingweight, which helps them avoid injuries like tennis elbow.

**Plugged In**

Hi-tech machines are part of sports announcer **Joe Buck**'s profession. But one of his coolest gadgets is the telestrator, which allows announcers to draw on the screen to demonstrate plays. Buck jokes that he is no master strategist, though. "We'll show some goofy fan, and I might draw on him to mess around," says Buck. "That's about as technical as I get."

VOLUME   PHASE   CHROMA   BRIGHT   CONTRAST

ON   OFF

POWER

1) Justin St.Pierre - unsportsmanlike
2) Chris Lee - charging
3) Rob Martell - spearing
4) Brad Meier - interference
5) Rob Shick - slashing
6) Bill McCreary - delayed penalty call
7) Tim Peel - cross-checking
8) Don VanMassenhoven - roughing
9) Kerry Fraser - hooking
10) Steve Miller - slow whistle
11) Dean Warren - goal signal
12) Dan O'Halloran - high stick
13) Brad Lazarowich - face off
14) Gord Dwyer - elbowing
15) Lyle Seitz - whistle for face off
16) Mark Wheler - wave offsides
17) Jean Morin - icing call
18) Brad Watson - no goal

# NEED FOR SPEED

**Vroom! Vroom!**
A motocross rider zooms past the crowd. Motocross races require riders to speed through the course, going over bumps and literally flying off of hills and jumps.

**Don't Blink . . .**

or you might miss the action. Drag racers can reach more than 300 miles per hour and a quarter-mile race can be finished in less than five seconds. The top-fuel cars are so powerful that they leave the starting line with as much force as a space shuttle.

### ◁ Fire on Ice

Speed skaters like **Kip Carpenter** wear aerodynamic suits and special skates that allow them to glide across the ice at speeds that can top 30 miles per hour. The fastest skaters can go 1,000 meters in just over a minute, which is about as fast as a greyhound can run.

### △ Last One's a Rotten Egg

Racers take off at the USA Track and Field Championships. In 1996, Michael Johnson set a world record when he ran 200 meters in an astounding 19.32 seconds. That means he was going 23 miles per hour. In some driving zones, he could've been pulled over for speeding!

**All Systems Go**

**John Force,** a drag racing legend, has 125 career victories. After completing the quickest Funny Car pass of his career, Force said, "Quickest don't win you championships and it don't win you races. But it sure makes you feel good."

41

**Yee-haw!**
In calf roping, a rider must lasso the calf, dismount his horse and tie the calf down – all while racing against the clock. The best ropers can finish in less than 10 seconds and the world record is less than 6 seconds.

**"If everything seems just not going fas**

**Unstoppable**
Guard **Allen Iverson** is one of the NBA's quickest players and best scorers. In 12 seasons, A.I. has scored almost 23,000 points and won the MVP award in 2001, the same year he led the Philadelphia 76ers to the NBA Finals.

nder control, you're
enough. **99**

— Mario Andretti, race car driver

**155**
**miles per hour** is the world-record speed of tennis star **Andy Roddick's** serve. That serve broke his old mark of 153 m.p.h. Not surprisingly, both of them went unreturned.

**83**

**miles per hour**

is the speed of submarine pitcher **Mike Myers'** fastball. While there's no official record of the fastest pitch ever thrown, some have been clocked at more than 100 m.p.h. Talk about feeling the heat.

**Hit the Brakes!**
There's no room for error in NASCAR, where the speedometers can top 200 miles per hour. The high-speed races are so dangerously fast that at some tracks, drivers must place restrictor plates on the engines to slow the cars down.

# PLAYING DIRTY

**Power Steering**
Steer wrestling is the quickest of all the rodeo events. A cowboy has to chase down the steer, jump off his horse and then wrestle the steer to the ground as fast as possible. The world record in the sport: 2.4 seconds.

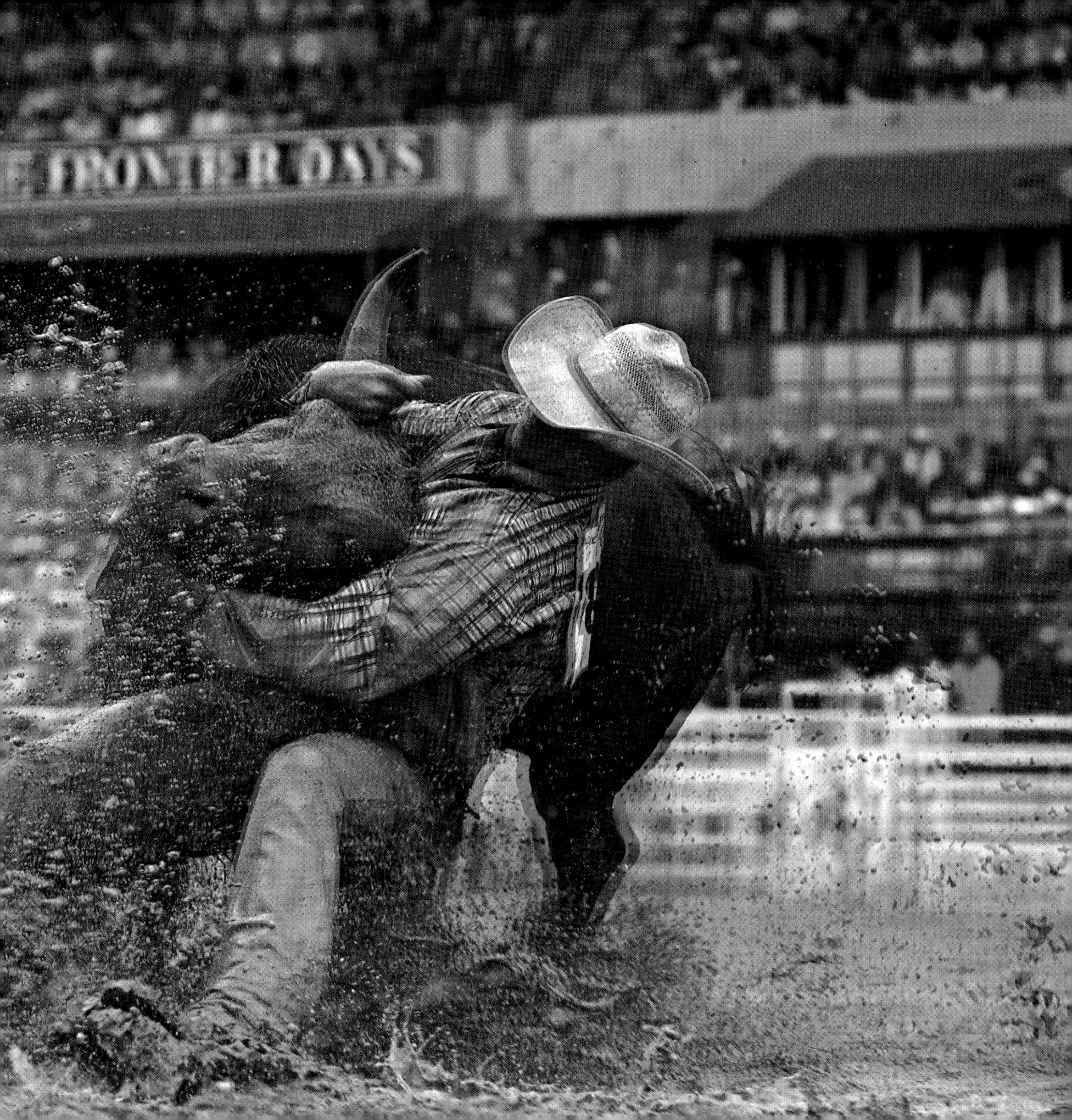
FRONTIER DAYS

▷ **Speed Racer**
Motocross rider **Ricky Carmichael**, who retired from the sport in 2007, is the self-proclaimed GOAT: Greatest Of All Time. He holds the American Motorcyclist Association record with 150 national wins

**❝There is an eagle in me that wants to soar, and there is a hippopotamus in me that wants to wallow in the mud.❞**

— Carl Sandburg, author

▷ **What a Mess!**
Competitors in the annual Mississippi mud volleyball tournament in Hannibal, Missouri get themselves in some sticky situations. The games take place next to a levee of the Mississippi River and are played on 60' x 30' courts filled with at least six inches of fresh Mississippi mud.

**Dirt Devils**
Did you know that the word motocross is derived from the words motorcycle and cross country? The sport has been in existence since the 1920s.

**Sand Storm**
The bunker may be a golfer's biggest nemesis, but there's a lot of thought put into the type of sand that goes into those traps. Sand with high amounts of gravel and coarse particles can damage mowers, hurt putting ability, and slow play on the golf course.

# Ooof!

▷ **Leap of Faith**
This track athlete took a bad dive, something that rarely happened to U.S. Olympian Mike Powell, the men's world record holder in the long jump. In 1991, he jumped 29' 4½".

### Hold Your Breath

Swimmers dive in for a race at the Olympics. There are
four types of strokes: butterfly, backstroke, breaststroke
and freestyle. Freestyle is regarded as the fastest.

# "I want to test my maximum and see how much I can do. And I want to change the world of swimming."

— Michael Phelps, Olympic gold medalist

**Golden Boy**

**Michael Phelps,** a 17-time world champion, is one of the greatest swimmers of all time. The 6' 4" Phelps set his first world record at age 15 to become the youngest man ever to break a world mark.

## Making Waves

World-record times have been decreasing as swimmers get faster and modern swimsuits reduce drag. The fastest swimmers can swim 200 meters in less than two minutes.

▷ **You Can Lead a Horse to Water...**

But he'd better get out quick. In the steeplechase, horses race through an obstacle course in which they jump over fences and run through pits of water.

## ▷ Taking Aim

The sport of water polo is a combination of lacrosse (without the sticks) and swimming. Teams try to get the ball across the pool and throw it into the opposing team's goal. Players swim up to one-and-a-half miles during a typical game.

## ▽ Slippery When Wet

Steeplechase is not just a horse race — it is also a track and field event. The typical course is almost two miles long with 28 obstacles and seven water jumps. The race dates back to the 1860s.

# COLD AS ICE

## Spray On

Detroit Red Wings winger **Kirk Maltby** has no trouble on his skates here, but NHL players are very sensitive to ice conditions. Many don't like playing in warm-weather cities because the heat and humidity can make the ice soft, slushy, and sticky.

**Didn't I Just Pass You?**
Snowboarding came naturally for Olympian **Nate Holland**, who is known for his intense, all-out style. "I've always loved the snow since I was a kid, he says. "And I love it especially now that it's a key ingredient in my profession."

# Go big or go home

> **"This is our canvas. Our easel. This is how we paint, on fresh sheets of ice."**
>
> — Jeremy Roenick, NHL center

**Perfect Strike**
**Mika Koivuniemi** has won eight
titles on the Pro Bowling Association
tour. The Finland native was also the
PBA Bowler of the Year in 2003-04.
And he did it all without bumpers!

**▷ Diving In**
Racquetball combines elements of tennis, handball, and squash. Players use racquets to hit rubber balls against walls and ceilings. It requires good hand-eye coordination, not to mention goggles to protect your eyes from the fast-flying balls.

**❝One advantage of bowling over golf is that you never lose a bowling ball.❞**

—Don Carter, pro bowler

**▷ Strings Attached**
**Ian Cole** is one of the top yo-yo artists in the country. He specializes in difficult off-string tricks and has been yo-yoing since he was 13.

### Airborne

Want to be a pilot without getting into a cockpit? You can fly a model! Gliders don't use motors and rely on lift forces to stay in the air. But some models need an engine, like the remote-controlled helicopter above.

ICHIRO SUZUKI

DAVID ORTIZ

MICKEY MANTLE

BOBBY COX

ALEX RODRIGUEZ

## ◁ Signature Style
The most prized possession for many fans: a player's autograph. Fans go to great lengths to get that scribble on a baseball, and sometimes that hard work pays off. In 2005, a Babe Ruth-signed baseball sold for $150,000!

**Jackpot**
Scott's a lucky guy. Not everyone gets a personally signed piece of lumber from one of the greatest sluggers of all time, **Albert Pujols.**

WRIGLEY FIELD
HOME OF
CHICAGO CUBS
NEXT CHICAGO CUBS
HOME GAMES:

355

### Take Me Out

Chicago Cubs fans are used to flooding Wrigley Field for day games. The ballpark with famed ivy-covered walls is the second oldest in the majors. Wrigley didn't install lights until 1988, making it the last major-league park to stage night games.

**Yanks a Lot**
New York Yankees fans aren't afraid to display their devotion to the Bronx Bombers on their chest — even when they're visiting the division rival Baltimore Orioles at Camden Yards.

# THE HARDWARE

"If winning isn't everything, why do they keep score?"

– Vince Lombardi

# Stanley Cup Champions

2006-07 - Anaheim Ducks
2005-06 - Carolina Hurricanes
2003-04 - Tampa Bay Lightning
2002-03 - New Jersey Devils
2001-02 - Detroit Red Wings
2000-01 - Colorado Avalanche
1999-2000 - New Jersey Devils
1998-99 - Dallas Stars
1997-98 - Detroit Red Wings
1996-97 - Detroit Red Wings
1995-96 - Colorado Avalanche
1994-95 - New Jersey Devils
1993-94 - New York Rangers
1992-93 - Montreal Canadiens
1991-92 - Pittsburgh Penguins
1990-91 - Pittsburgh Penguins
1989-90 - Edmonton Oilers
1988-89 - Calgary Flames
1987-88 - Edmonton Oilers
1986-87 - Edmonton Oilers
1985-86 - Montreal Canadiens
1984-85 - Edmonton Oilers
1983-84 - Edmonton Oilers
1982-83 - New York Islanders
1981-82 - New York Islanders
1980-81 - New York Islanders
1979-80 - New York Islanders
1978-79 - Montreal Canadiens
1977-78 - Montreal Canadiens
1976-77 - Montreal Canadiens
1975-76 - Montreal Canadiens
1974-75 - Philadelphia Flyers
1973-74 - Philadelphia Flyers
1972-73 - Montreal Canadiens
1971-72 - Boston Bruins
1970-71 - Montreal Canadiens
1969-70 - Boston Bruins
1968-69 - Montreal Canadiens
1967-68 - Montreal Canadiens

1966-67 - Toronto Maple Leafs
1962-63 - Toronto Maple Leafs
1961-62 - Toronto Maple Leafs
1960-61 - Chicago Blackhawks
1959-60 - Montreal Canadiens
1958-59 - Montreal Canadiens
1957-58 - Montreal Canadiens
1956-57 - Montreal Canadiens
1955-56 - Montreal Canadiens
1954-55 - Detroit Red Wings
1953-54 - Detroit Red Wings
1952-53 - Montreal Canadiens
1951-52 - Detroit Red Wings
1950-51 - Toronto Maple Leafs
1949-50 - Detroit Red Wings
1948-49 - Toronto Maple Leafs
1947-48 - Toronto Maple Leafs
1946-47 - Toronto Maple Leafs
1945-46 - Montreal Canadiens
1944-45 - Toronto Maple Leafs
1943-44 - Montreal Canadiens
1942-43 - Detroit Red Wings
1941-42 - Toronto Maple Leafs
1940-41 - Boston Bruins
1939-40 - New York Rangers
1938-39 - Boston Bruins
1937-38 - Chicago Black Hawks
1936-37 - Detroit Red Wings
1935-36 - Detroit Red Wings
1934-35 - Montreal Maroons
1933-34 - Chicago Black Hawks
1932-33 - New York Rangers
1931-32 - Toronto Maple Leafs
1930-31 - Montreal Canadiens
1929-30 - Montreal Canadiens
1928-29 - Boston Bruins
1927-28 - New York Rangers
1926-27 - Ottawa Senators

▷ **High and Mighty**
Anaheim Ducks goalie
**Jean-Sebastien Giguere**
hoists the Stanley Cup after
backstopping his team
to victory in 2007. The
Ducks were the first team
from California to win the
famous trophy, which has
been awarded to the NHL
champions since 1927.

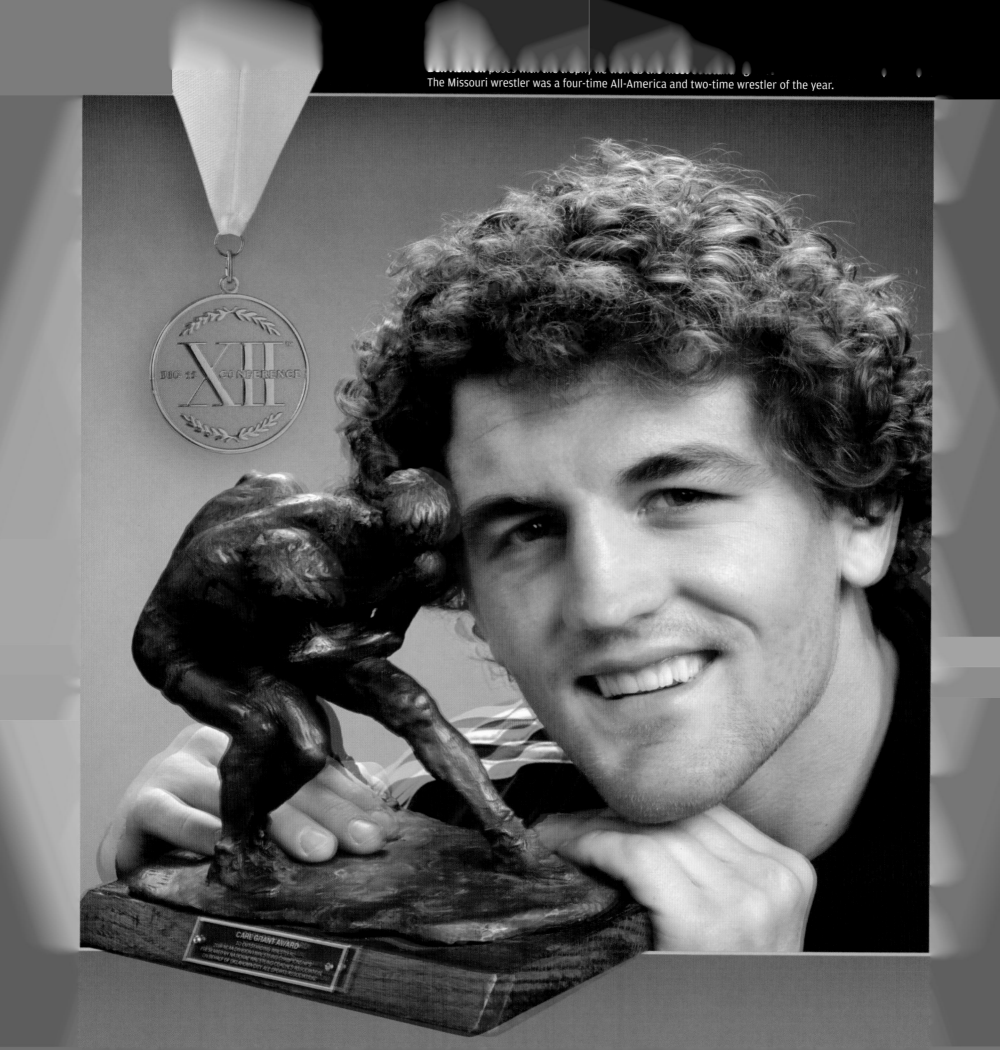

**Brett Favre** won Super Bowl XXXI with the Green Bay Packers and led them back to the Super Bowl the following year.

**Kurt Warner** was named Super Bowl MVP in 2000 after his St. Louis Rams beat the Tennessee Titans for the championship.

**Peyton Manning** and the Indianapolis Colts beat the Chicago Bears in Super Bowl XLI. Manning was named Super Bowl MVP.

**Tom Brady** of the New England Patriots has been to four Super Bowls, winning three, and taking home the MVP award twice.

## Cardinals Rule

St. Louis Cardinals pitcher **Adam Wainwright** celebrates his team's 2006 World Series victory. Despite winning only 83 games during the regular season, the Cardinals beat the Detroit Tigers in five games for the championship. Wainwright won a game and saved another. He struck out Brandon Inge for the last out in the Series.

# BAD BREAKS

**Swat Team**

NBA teams are out of luck when they run into **Marcus Camby** (23) in the paint. Camby is a shot blocking specialist. A former NBA defensive player of the year, the 6'11" center led the league in blocked shots in 2006-07 and 2007-08.

▷ **Steamed**
This motocross rider was left standing when his bike broke down. Engines fail when they overheat or don't have enough lubrication.

**Back on His Feet**
It takes a brave cowboy to ride a four-legged beast like a bull. A bull rider must ride the animal with one hand for eight seconds. That is, if the 2,200 pound bull doesn't buck the rider into the mud first.

# bummer . . .

### ◁ Slip 'n Slide
Even with a good leap, runners in the 3,000-meter steeplechase get wet. A fall in a water jump is quite the soaker!

### Great Comeback
What's a little roll in a rally car? British champion **Colin McRae** turned upside down, but recovered and finished this X Games race.

## Heads Up!
A wheel flies off the humongous Grave Digger. Monster trucks generally crush everything in their path, but sometimes they run into trouble of their own.

**We Have Liftoff**

Whether you're making a mid-air catch, leaping gracefully, flying above a halfpipe or soaring toward the basket, sometimes you have to leave the ground. Take a look at these athletes who defy gravity.

# Up,

**Rip Hamilton** of the Detroit Pistons shoots over the San Antonio Spurs' **Tony Parker** and **Manu Ginobili**.

# up,

Utah Jazz forward **Carlos Boozer** can't quite reach this towering shot by **David West** of the New Orleans Hornets.

# and away!

Utah's **Mehmet Okur** floats in the air before shooting against West.

◁ **A Big Hit**
**Jeff Francoeur** is used to having the ball fly off his bat. After all, he slammed a three-run homer in his first major league at bat. In his first three seasons with the Atlanta Braves, Francoeur hit 62 homers and won a Gold Glove award.

**He's the Manning**
Think fast. This pass from **Peyton Manning** is coming your way. He has thrown 275 TDs in nine seasons, including a then-record 49 in 2004.

**Get Outta Here!**
It was an air battle between two of the WNBA's biggest stars when Indiana Fever defensive whiz **Tamika Catchings** faced off against Detroit Shock forward **Cheryl Ford.**

**Air Ball**
In a college basketball game against Valparaiso, this Ole Miss player reaches new heights as he goes for the ball.

66 **Flying is learning how to throw yourself at the ground and miss.** 99

— Douglas Adams, writer

**Flippin' and Fishin'**
The University of Missouri's **Jason Miller** shows off his hops in the high jump at a track and field meet. Meanwhile, fly fisherman **Greg Horn** aims for precise placement of the fly to catch rainbow trout.

## △ Show-stopper

Goalkeeper **Tim Howard** goes airborne to block a shot. While playing with Manchester United in 2004, Howard became the first American to win the FA Cup.

## △ A Lot of Hot Air

Heated gas allow these hot air balloons to stay afloat. In 1999, two adventurers traveled around the world in a hot air balloon, completing the trip in 19 days, 21 hours.

### Plan of Attack

New England Patriots quarterback **Tom Brady** passes over the Buffalo Bills defense. In his dominant 2007 MVP season, Brady broke the single-season touchdown record (50) while leading his Patriots to a perfect 16-0 record.

**"The illusion of space is what 3-D pictures are all about. I hope you've enjoyed exploring this universe of stereoscopic images . . . The world of 3-D is right at your fingertips."**

– DDDavid E. Klutho